Real Dragons

By Jordan Avery

Contents

Dragons

Dragons are real!

Not flying dragons from made-up stories, but some reptiles!

Komodo Dragon

A Komodo dragon is a giant reptile.

These reptiles are longer than a lion!
They eat a diet of meat, like wild pigs and other animals.

If you happen to meet one of these dragons, you might have a problem.

Don't take a sudden step!

They can run quite fast, and they can ruin your day!

But you can relax!

Komodo dragons are located in just one remote place on the planet.

Bearded Dragon

A bearded dragon has spikes along its body to protect itself.

The flap under its jaws looks like a beard!

These dragons live in the desert.

They do not drink a lot of fluids.

Their diet includes insects, spiders and plants.

Frilled Dragon

Frilled dragons use a great method for staying safe.

They react to bigger animals by flicking out the frill around their necks!

This frill makes the dragon look big and mad.

Bigger animals get a fright and run away!

What a triumph!

Water Dragon

Water dragons have a talent for swimming in rivers!

But these dragons walk on land, too.
They walk and run on long back legs.

Earless Dragon

Earless dragons have no ears.

We thought they might be extinct, but then we found one and took photos!

These dragons can be quite small.

This baby dragon is tiny!

Now you know dragons are real!

These reptiles don't fly or spew flames, but they are dragons.

CHECKING FOR MEANING

1. What does a bearded dragon's diet include? *(Literal)*
2. How does the frilled dragon scare other animals? *(Literal)*
3. How might a Komodo dragon ruin your day? *(Inferential)*
4. Which of the dragons in this book is most like a dragon from a fantasy story? Why? *(Evaluative)*

EXTENDING VOCABULARY

reptile	What is a reptile? How are reptiles different from other animals? What do you think their skin feels like?
remote	What does the word *remote* mean in the text? Do Komodo dragons live somewhere close to other places or far away?
extinct	What is the difference between an animal or plant being dead and being extinct?

MOVING BEYOND THE TEXT

1. Which dragon in the text is your favourite? Why?
2. What are some animals that are extinct? How can we stop other animals, such as the earless dragon, from becoming extinct?
3. Bearded dragons live in the desert and don't need much water. What other animals live in the desert? What other animals don't need much water?
4. If you could have one of the special features of the dragons in the text, which would you choose? Why?

TIME TO WRITE

Choose one dragon from the book and write about a day in its life. What does it do? What does it eat?